The Shepherd's Trail

The Shepherd's Trail

Cat Urbigkit

Boyds Mills Press
Honesdale, Pennsylvania

To all the shepherds of the world, especially my friends from Nepal
—C.U.

The author wishes to thank Cherubim A. Quizon, Ph.D., Department of Sociology
and Anthropology, Seton Hall University, for reviewing the author's note on page 32.

Boyds Mills Press, Inc.
815 Church Street
Honesdale, Pennsylvania 18431
Printed in China

Library of Congress Cataloging-in-Publication Data

Urbigkit, Cat.
  The shepherd's trail / Cat Urbigkit. — 1st ed.
    p. cm.
  ISBN 978-1-59078-509-6 (hardcover : alk. paper)
  1. Sheep—West (U.S.)—Juvenile literature. 2. Shepherds—West (U.S.)—Juvenile literature.
  3. Sheepherding—West (U.S.)—Juvenile literature. I. Title.

  SF375.2.U73 2008
  636.300978—dc22
                            2007017475

First edition
The text of this book is set in 14-point Minion.

10 9 8 7 6 5 4 3 2 1

O N A QUIET, SAGEBRUSH-COVERED RIDGE
in a Wyoming desert sits a sheep wagon. It's a relic from years gone by,
but wagons such as this one still play an important role on a working
sheep ranch. Shepherds continue to live in these wagons, tending
their flocks on the western trail. Today, the wagons have rubber tires
instead of wooden wheels. But scenes like this have been a part of the
landscape of the American West for over one hundred years.

DOMESTIC SHEEP GRAZE IN MIGRATORY FLOCKS on rangelands throughout the western United States, moving with the seasons. The sheep are raised for both meat and wool production. After spending summer in the high mountains, many flocks migrate to lower elevations in the winter. The sheep spend the cold season in the sagebrush desert, living on largely unfenced land, far from urban areas.

WINTER SNOWS IN THE DESERT PROVIDE NEEDED moisture for the sheep, and the snow is usually shallow enough so sheep can dig for vegetation to eat. The distance from the winter to summer range is usually between one hundred fifty and two hundred fifty miles. In a process called trailing, some ranchers let their herds slowly walk to the new range, grazing along the way. Other ranchers truck their herds, as seen here.

EACH HERD, OR BAND, OF SHEEP IS HANDLED by one or two sheepherders hired by the ranch owner. Bands of female sheep, called ewes, consist of one thousand to two thousand sheep. Bands of male sheep, called rams, are smaller, since ranchers usually keep one ram per twenty-five ewes.

Many sheepherders hired to tend sheep in the American West come from sheepherding cultures. They include Mexicans, Basques, Native Americans, Mongolians, and Nepalese. Sheepherders, also called shepherds, live quiet but busy lives, free from modern conveniences such as computers and telephones. They live with the herds year-round. Riding on horseback, they move the sheep to each grazing area and bedding ground with the help of herding dogs. A bedding ground is the place where the herd stops to sleep for the night.

E<small>ACH FALL,</small> as sheep come down from the mountains, sheep ranchers sort their herds.

They send lambs that were born that spring to market and prepare the remaining animals for the coming winter.

RANCHERS USE A variety of tools to manage their sheep, and herding dogs are among the most important, no matter what the season.

Herding dogs are used to sort and move sheep. Bred just for this type of work, they have a natural instinct for the job. The dogs are trained to respond to verbal commands, whistles, or hand signals.

Border collies, Australian shepherds, and bearded collies are breeds of herding dogs. Abe, shown here, is a bearded collie.

THESE SHEEP BELONG to the Arambel family and will soon begin a two-hundred-mile migration, which will take months of walking and grazing, from mountains to desert.

These sheep belong to the Thoman family. The sheep will be trucked from the mountains to the Thoman ranch, about one hundred miles away, for the winter.

THE EWE FLOCKS SPEND THEIR DAYS GRAZING and resting, preparing for the upcoming breeding season. Range sheep have strong flocking instincts, meaning they like to stay close together. That makes herding easier than with other types of sheep that may not have the flocking behavior. Flocking also serves as protection against predators.

THE SHEEP RISE EARLY. They stretch and begin to graze away from the bedding area soon after sunrise. After a few hours, the sheep will lie down to rest, loafing during the hot hours of the day.

The sheep will graze again in midafternoon, then settle down on fresh bedding ground before the sun sets in the evening. Sheep usually bed high on a hill or ridge, where they can see for long distances and feel safe.

THE SHEEPERDER TENDS
the herd all day, from dawn to dusk,
slowly moving the sheep to grazing
areas, water, and the bedding ground.
Once the sheep are safely bedded down
in the evening, the herder can return to
his wagon to prepare his evening meal.
He leaves guardian dogs to keep watch
over the herd during the night.

GUARDIAN DOGS LIVE with the sheep, protecting them from predators, such as coyotes and bears. The dogs patrol the herd and will bark at and attack any predator approaching the flock.

Guardian dogs are raised with lambs in a process called socialization or bonding. Deep affection develops between the dog and the sheep in the herd.

THE EWES ARE NOT THE ONLY ONES getting ready for breeding season. The rams have been growing strong and healthy. They are kept separated from the ewes until breeding time. The rams stay together in what is called a ram band or buck band. Ranchers sort the rams to check their health and quality before they are turned in with the ewes.

THE DROP IN TEMPERATURE, along with the first snowfall, means breeding time has arrived. The rams are let into the ewe flock in December. They will breed the ewes and stay with them until it's shearing time in the spring.

Winters on the high desert are commonly dry and cold, but occasional fierce blizzards can isolate the sheepherders and threaten the flocks. The sheep usually seek brushy hillsides for shelter, and their wool provides protection from the bitter cold.

IN AREAS WHERE THE SNOW is too deep for the sheep to graze, the sheep are fed hay. The snow provides a clean plate for each meal.

Other sheep thrive on native forage that grows in the high sagebrush desert. Grazing lands are carefully managed by ranchers, so there is plenty of food for both livestock and wildlife. Healthy animals can be raised only on healthy range.

OUT ON THE RANGE, herders depend on their sheep wagons, which were invented in the 1880s. The wagons contain everything a herder needs, including a bed, stove, table, and storage.

Every sheep camp also has a commissary wagon. Extra supplies are kept in the wagon, including corn for the sheep, hay for the horses, and food for the dogs.

The ranch owner commonly serves as camptender. The camptender's job includes bringing supplies and mail to the camp as well as directing the herder where to move next on the range. The camptender helps move the sheepherder's camp every few days.

AS WINTER RECEDES, the snow begins to melt and temperatures rise, giving way to spring and shearing time. Shearing is completed before spring lambing begins. Getting rid of their long wool coats allows the sheep to tolerate warmer weather in the summer, but it also makes it easier for lambs to find their mothers' milk. For shearing, sheep are moved into corrals, where the rams and pregnant ewes are placed in separate bands until the next breeding season.

A TEAM OF professional sheepshearers arrives on the ranch to do the job. The shearers bring portable shearing plants, which contain mechanical shears and power generators to run them.

Shearing is a busy time on the ranch. Each sheep is carefully handled. Professional shearers take only about three minutes to shear each sheep. The wool comes off each sheep in one large bundle, called fleece.

WOOL IS SORTED ACCORDING TO QUALITY AND stuffed into bales that weigh about four hundred pounds. The long fine wool from these Rambouillet (*ram-boo-lay*) sheep is used to make wool clothing. Coarse wool, which is too scratchy for clothes, is used to make wool rugs. The wool is sent on trucks to a buyer or wool warehouse, where it will be sold and shipped all over the world.

F OR EVERY ONE HUNDRED WHITE SHEEP,
the rancher puts a black sheep into the flock, or the rancher may paint
a white sheep a dark color using a marking fluid that doesn't harm the
wool. This sheep is called a marker sheep. If a marker sheep is missing,
the herder knows some sheep are missing. Ten marker sheep means
there are one thousand sheep in the herd. If only nine markers are
counted, that means the herder needs to look for missing sheep.

SOME SHEEP WEAR BELLS AROUND THEIR NECKS.
If the sheep are moving, the sheepherder can hear the bells, even
if it is dark outside or if it is snowing too hard to see the animals.
The sheepherder can locate the sheep as long as the sound of
the bells is within hearing distance. If the bells ring quickly in the
night, when sheep should be asleep, that could mean a predator is
chasing the sheep and they need the herder's help. Sheep bells are
removed before shearing, then placed back on the shorn sheep.

LAMBING TIME COMES WITH GREEN GRASS,
warmer temperatures, and freshly shorn ewes. Five months after being
bred, ewes will give birth to their lambs, usually single lambs or twins,
although triplets are not uncommon. Within minutes, these tiny
white lambs are standing up to nurse while their mother cleans them,
stimulating the lambs' blood circulation at the same time.

SOMETIMES A LAMB
will become separated from its
mother, or the ewe dies and the
lamb becomes an orphan. The
rancher or herder takes the orphan
lambs to the ranch, where they
are hand-raised. Bottle feeding
lambs is fun, and these lambs often
become ranch-yard pets.

SHEEP RANCHERS HAVE TO TAKE CARE OF
their animals' health. The animals are routinely vaccinated against
disease and treated for internal and external parasites.

Lambs must also have their long tails shortened, in a process called
docking. Docking helps ensure that manure does not accumulate on the
tail, which could eventually make the sheep sick.

This box contains veterinary tools and supplies used on a sheep ranch.

THE EWE FLOCK, once it is finished lambing, is moved to the high summer range. Mountain forage provides lots of nutrition for the ewes and helps them make milk for their babies. The result is big, healthy lambs. Good food and overall animal health affect the quality of the wool.

L AMBS GROW QUICKLY. W HEN FALL ARRIVES, they are ready to be separated from their mothers. Sorting is done when the flocks return from the mountains. All the male lambs are sent to market, while the females are grouped together to form a ewe-lamb flock, ready to hit the grazing trail, as their mothers did before them. The ewe lambs will continue to grow and will eventually become the mothers of the next generation of lambs that follow the shepherd's trail.

AUTHOR'S NOTE

Moving animal herds from low elevations to high elevations is a practice known as transhumance. This practice requires space, and there is plenty of space in the American West. Some people call this part of the United States the Empty Interior. The huge area spans the eastern slopes of the Rocky Mountains to the eastern border of California, from the Canadian border to the Mexican border. This area has extreme geography, with high plateaus, dry deserts, river valleys, flatlands, steep canyons, and rugged mountains. Much of the land is classified as public land. People are allowed to use the land for activities such as livestock grazing, recreation, and mining.

Few people reside in the Empty Interior compared with the rest of the United States. People live on farms and ranches or in small communities. A handful of cities are scattered within the region, too. Generally, there are more cattle and sheep per square mile than there are people. It's in this part of the West where herders practice transhumance.

During the winter, animals stay at lower elevations (deserts). This is usually where the herders have permanent homes. During warmer seasons, the animals move to higher elevations (mountains), accompanied by their herders, who stay in temporary shelters.

Transhumance has been practiced for thousands of years and occurs throughout the world.